D1343540

more BRAIN BUILDING *Games*

GEDDES & GROSSET

This edition published 2010 by Geddes & Grosset
144 Port Dundas Road, Glasgow, G4 0HZ, Scotland

First Published 2001 by Brainwaves Books, a Division of Allen D. Bragdon Publishers, Inc.,
252 Great Western Road, South Yarmouth, MA 02664

Copyright © 2001 by Allen D. Bragdon Publishers, Inc.

All rights reserved. No part of this book may be reproduced in any manner whatsoever
without the written permission of the publisher

Design and editorial production: Carolyn Zellers. Exercise editing: Wallace Exman. Puzzle
graphics formatting: David Zellers. Performance Tips text rewrite: Melissa Pendleton.
Proofreader: Vida Morris

Drawings by Malcolm Wells

This book is the second of two books and contains explanatory material that is common to
both. Some puzzle concepts were first published in a column called " Playspace" that was
created by Allen Bragdon in the 1980s for global syndication by *The New York Times*.

Some images copyright © 2001 www.arttoday.com. Some images reproduced with permission
of LifeArt Collection Images, copyright © 1989-99 TechPOOL Studios, Cleveland, OH.

ISBN 978-1-84205-656-1

Printed in the UK

Contents

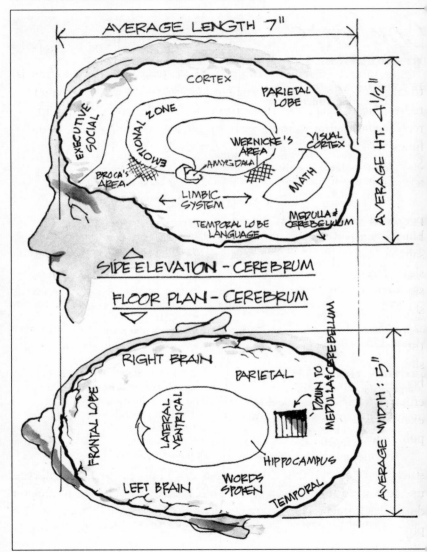

C ongratulations! You have decided to take charge of your brain's future. That is the hard part. Our contribution to that effort is to create exercises in interesting puzzle formats. We are also going to tell you how the six cognitive systems that work hardest for you in real-world situations can be made to do their best work. We call these functions the *Executive, Memory, Computation, Spatial, Language* and *Social/Emotional*. Those are the ones that make you excel at work, build a useful store of memories, plan for and live an interesting old age.

Permit us some straight talk about your second most valuable possession. Your brain began to slow down as soon as its original blueprint finished unfolding in your mid-20s. It has lost capacity at the same rate every year since, and it will continue to do so. Symptoms of slowing down — from "senior moments" to Alzheimer's — are simply signs of the cumulative effects of continuing loss that have begun to show up in your outward behaviour.

The good news is that you can *do* something about that. You took the first step when you picked up this book. It is designed to help you slow down the slowing down. There are no pills or vaccines yet to boost your intelligence with no effort. In the future some memory-enhancing pills will be tested, approved and sold. Now, targeted exercise is as good for your brain as for your muscles and cardiopulmonary systems.

Try one exercise each day. Start with the easy ones. If you get stuck, don't quit on that exercise. Use the "Hint" printed in small type, upside down at the bottom of the page. Rotate from chapter to chapter during each week. Think of that daily routine as being like sets of physical exercises for different muscle-groups. When you have finished the book try one of the first ones you did again. Even if you have forgotten the answer you will be surprised at how easy it seems.

Each day you will be able to learn something about how the human brain works when it solves problems. We call these performance tips "didjaknows" because many of them will come as a surprise. Yet we have selected them from cutting-edge neuroscientific research results, many of them from research published since the millennium. Often you can apply them directly to real life situations to improve performance. Some will confirm a sense you have had all along, on your own, about how the brain gets things done. Together, the exercises and the performance tips will help you in three, quite different, ways. First, they will make you more effectively aware that you can actually control much of what goes on in your brain. You can improve the hand you were dealt. Second, they will teach you strategies for seeing problems in ways that suggest solutions. The different puzzle formats can be applied to real-world problems. Third, you will be growing stronger brain cells. Yes, when you make cells work they will physically grow new connectors, called *dendrites* and *axons*, that allow them to pass along signals from cell to cell. Like anything else, the more resources you can bring to bear on a problem, the more likely you are to find a good solution.

And speaking of solutions, they are all there in the back of the book. Forget about our solution until you have finished the puzzle *your* way. A major reason for sticking with a puzzle until you have mastered it, painful as it may be, is that it benefits you in the same way "no pain, no gain" does in a physical exercise routine. It builds up the same kind of stamina. It's known as "concentration" in mental performance.

Perseverance can be improved in the same way that aerobic training equips you to run or swim longer and longer each time. Often, superior concentration powers will win a competitive race to a solution.

A few housekeeping points:

We first created most of the puzzle formats in this book of mental exercises for a daily column requested by *The New York Times* to syndicate outside the United States in the 1980s. We called it "Playspace" and meant it. Play is an essential activity to further learning. Consider the most ferociously productive period of learning in your own life. Between the ages of two and six you taught yourself the grammar and vocabulary of a language you had never heard before. You learned the rules of right and wrong in a confused society. You stood up, risked gravity and walked forward. You moved from convenience to duty when you bought into potty training. That's a lot to accomplish in four years. The whole time you were playing, or so it seemed to all those huge people around you who were busy doing important things with their lives. You were really studying them like laboratory animals that fed *you*, picking up clues as fast as your neurons could scamper. Long live a light and eager heart!

For most of our mature lives, David and I have been joyfully engaged in learning how the human brain works its miracles — and devising tasks for it. We hope we have chosen well enough to captivate your interest and entertain your neurons while they stretch.

— Allen Bragdon

Section One
EXECUTIVE

The *Executive Function* in the human brain is located in the frontal part of the forehead above the eyes. This area has evolved after the other areas of the primate brain. It is also the last to mature in children and does not fully develop until after the age of nine. Some neurophysiologists even claim it is not fully developed until the early 20s — a view also held by many parents based on their empirical evidence. As in the L.I.F.O. (Last In, First Out) system of inventory management, its accumulated bundle of human skills tends to be the first to deteriorate with age.

Executive thinking tools are comprised of cleverly-designed devices. One such device is *Working Memory* which holds data in mind temporarily while the brain manipulates it. Notice, for example, how you multiply 89 x 91 in your head. Or read the following sentence and answer the question that appears on the next page. "The waitress asked her assistant to clear the blue dishes but leave the bread basket for the bartender to take home to his parrot."

Business executives are, or should be, skilled at visualizing possible future paths for the firm and charting the intermediate steps required to achieve the chosen goal. As new data emerges, the executive must adapt original strategies without sacrificing the goal.

Accordingly, Executive Functions include the capacity to alter responses to adjust to new data. The brain can adapt responses productively as the patterns of incoming data change, while still keeping the original goal in mind. *Einstellung* is the German word used by neuropsychologists to identify a mind set that cannot spot a new trend in a stream of data. Those minds continue to respond in an unproductive manner.

Many of the mental exercises in this section utilize *convergent* logic skills in which the working memory examines the data presented and works out the only correct conclusion. (Data: *Socrates is a man. All men are mortal.* Conclusion: *Socrates is mortal.*)

Divergent Intelligence, on the other hand, equips the mind to spot unfamiliar patterns. Often, they are newly forming within familiar data. It is also processed in the prefrontal area where Executive Functions reside. In many senses it is the anthesis of the *Einstellung* mind set. Interestingly, if the frontal area of the brain is damaged, convergent thinking skills are lost but the IQ remains unchanged. (Who wanted the bread basket?)

As the brain ages, the ability to manipulate data quickly with the Working Memory tool slows down. In fact it begins losing its edge when the brain has become fully mature in the early 20s. The rate of loss stays constant into old age but the cumulative effect commonly does not show up until "senior moments" begin to occur in the 60s.

The good news is that most Executive Function skills can be maintained by using them — working on the mental exercises in this book, for example. Because this galaxy of skills is essential to the highest levels of thinking, of insight and of productive behaviour, they are worth cultivating lifelong to maintain the highest quality of life.

Domi-Rows

DIRECTIONS

Convert these eight domino equations to numbers. A domino placed vertically denotes a fraction or division. If the domino is placed horizontally, the pips are added. One horizontal domino above another also signifies a fraction or division of the total number of pips. A blank is zero.

Didjaknow... THE MALE BRAIN AGES FASTER

When compared with women, men not only have a proportionately higher percent of white matter in their brain, they also have more fluid in their brain. Every time a brain cell dies it is replaced with cerebrospinal fluid. The amount of fluid in the brain indicates brain atrophy or death of brain cells. Anatomically, as men age, they loose brain tissue at about three times the rate of women. As for actual brain function, men between the ages of 18 and 45 increasingly lose their capacity to pay attention effectively on all ability tests, but especially those involving verbal memory. Women did not show any decline in this age group.

Answer on page 107

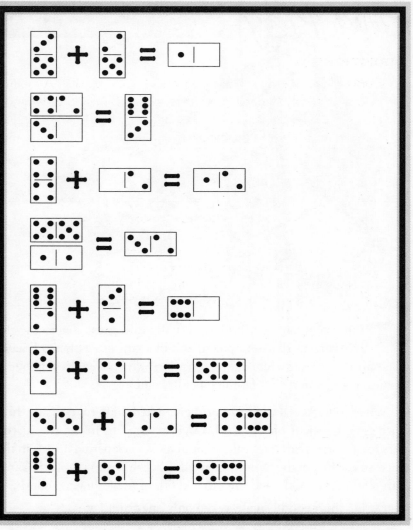

HINT: A whole number divided by 1 remains the same.

Fowl Play

From Monday to Friday, David diligently oversees the Department of Development and Plucking at Feathered Friends International. It's a demanding position which requires frequent business trips around FFI's far-flung poultry empire.

When the Accounting Department asked him to estimate how much time he spent on the road, David referred to his fourth-quarter diary for a recent year. It revealed that in a six-week period he was in the office on the first of the month, then the 4th, 8th, 9th, 11th, 12th, 22nd, 25th, 28th, 29th, 30th, and the 4th and 8th of the following month.

During this period David worked only one Saturday.

Answer on page 107

Can you figure out which days of the week David reported to his office during those six weeks? If you can, then you won't have any trouble discovering which months he referred to in his diary.

Didjaknow... **FEMALES AND MALES BOTH MENTALLY FLEXIBLE**

Healthy humans of both sexes do equally well on abstraction and flexibility tests (ABF tests). ABF tests measure the ability to create concepts out of images or examples and the ability to shift previous concepts to new ones when the images are shifted. On a battery of tests, men and women were asked to guess the category by which to sort certain objects. As the category changed during testing, both sexes realized the category shifted and applied new principles to the sorting task. Difficulties in ABF, however, can occur in either sex if there is damage sustained to the front part of the brain called the frontal lobe.

HINT: Sketch a seven-day calendar grid for six weeks and fill in the blanks.

Middle C's

DIRECTIONS

Opposite are two rows of three numbers each. Can you figure out the logical sequence of these numbers and fill in the final box in the third row?

Didjaknow... RAPID RESPONSE TO STROKE CAN SAVE YOUR LIFE

Strokes occur when blood flow to brain cells is blocked, frequently due to a clot in a blood vessel of the brain (ischaemic stroke) or, less often, by haemorrhage of a vessel. In minutes, brain cells die and brain damage begins. Fortunately, there is a drug treatment called T.P.A. (tissue plasminogen activator) that can break up a clot, but it must be administered within three hours of the onset of a stroke. Symptoms of stroke include numbness or weakness on one side of the body, confusion or trouble speaking, sudden vision problems, dizziness or loss of balance, or severe unexplained headache. If you suspect an impending stroke, you only have a short time to act. Do not delay. Call an ambulance immediately so treatment can begin.

Answer on page 107

A	B	C
108	356	124
196	780	292
284	648	

HINT: Work horizontally. Do something to A and B to find a relationship with C.

Astro-Logical

DIRECTIONS

If you've ever counted stars at night, here's a star-stumper to keep you busy. Twenty stars have been placed in the white squares, opposite, two stars in each horizontal and each vertical row. Can you place 20 more stars in the remaining empty squares? The catch: Only four stars are allowed in each horizontal and vertical row. Like most of life, there is more than one solution.

Didjaknow...

MEN "FIGHT OR FLEE"; WOMEN "TEND AND BEFRIEND"

Studies on male rats indicate that crowding increases stress because it elevates the stress hormone cortisol. With female rats, the reverse effect occurs: crowding appears to calm them. In humans, men tend to seek seclusion on arriving home from work and prefer to be left alone. If men have been under stress all day at work, they are more likely to provoke conflict within the family. In contrast, women under work-related stress, upon returning home, are more likely to cope by concentrating on their children. Studies show that even when women are under attack, they are more likely to protect their children and seek help from other females rather than fight and take flight.

Answer on page 107

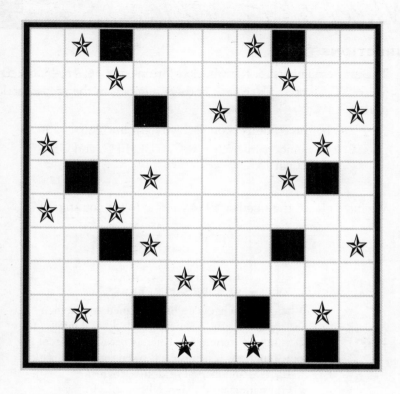

HINT: The four stars in the bottom row will stand side-by-side.

Wheel of Fortune

DIRECTIONS

The magic numbers for the wheel of fortune are: 34, 42, 43, 50, 51, 52, 59, 60, and 68. Place each of these numbers in the proper circle so that:

1. The three numbers on each straight line equal 153.
2. The numbers in circles ABC, CDE, EFG, and GHA also equal 153.

We have placed the number 59 in a circle to get you started.

Didjaknow...
ABILITY TESTS SHOW GENDER DIFFERENCES

When a group of over a hundred men and women underwent a battery of neuropsychological function tests, sex differences immediately became apparent in some functions. The results showed that on tests of abstraction and mental flexibility, there was no significant difference between males and females. When it came to face memory and verbal memory, both immediate and delayed, women did significantly better than men. However, on tests of motor skill and spatial ability, men performed noticeably better than women.

Answer on page 107

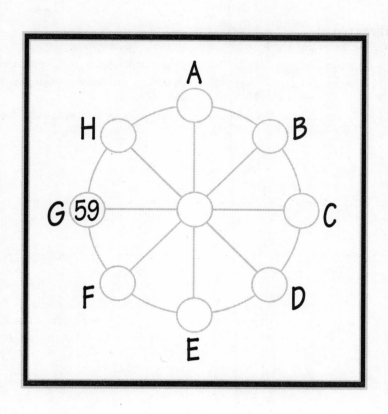

HINT: The number in the centre circle is 51.

CITATIONS

P. 12, 15, 20 Gur, Ruben C. Sex Differences in Learning. Using Brain Research to Reshape Classroom Practice. Public Information Resources, Inc. 7-9 November.

P. 16 Cheresh, David, et al, Scripps Research Institute and others at Henry Ford Health Sciences Center, "Nature Medicine" (2001).

P. 18 S.E. Taylor et al. (2000). Biobehavioral Responses to Stress in Females: Tend-and-Befriend, Not Fight-or-Flight. Psychological Review 107/3: 411-29.

Section Two
MEMORY

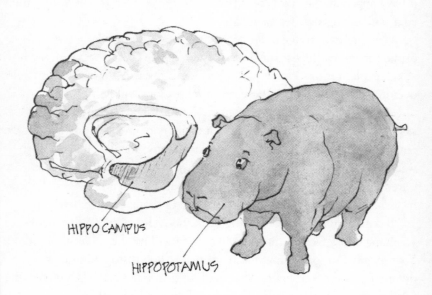

HIPPOCAMPUS

HIPPOPOTAMUS

This is about memory(s), plural, because the brain uses many different strategies to store data, retrieve it and distort it. If you know something about how these systems work you can tap the brain's built-in memory systems strategies to devise the best strategy each time.

Explicit memory (sometimes called *declarative* memory) is the kind you use when you consciously make an effort to remember something. Your brain stores *implicit, nondeclarative*, memories without your even knowing it has happened, much less being aware of trying. That is how you learned your native language, for example.

Here are two strategies for converting new data into long term explicit memory. Repeat the data in different ways: write it down, say it aloud, explain it to someone else, diagram it. Let it rest a while, then go over it again. Spacing out those rehearsal sessions will help.

Another method of learning new data is to steal a trick from your implicit memory system. Your implicit memory of an event (called *episodic* memory) becomes permanent because it was emotionally charged — your wedding day, an accident or the name of your first lover, for example. Often you can artificially apply an emotional "tag" to otherwise dull facts by associating them with some other weird or dramatic memory.

Relate all new data to existing memories. The more familiar hooks you hang a new fact on the more likely you will be able to recall it. Why? Your memory of something that happened to you is stored in many different parts of your brain. The smells of it in one place, the colours, the touch sensations, the sounds of it all in different arrays of cells. When you recall it, any one of those components can trigger the brain to go around and collect all the others to reconstruct the richness of the whole event. When you try to commit a description of an "event" to memory, say a date in history or a list of criteria for a diagnosis, create as many possible "triggers" as you can by visualizing the "event" in association with many different senses and familiar places or other events.

Strategies are important if you want to improve memory skills because practice does not help. Where practice does help is to lengthen the time you can concentrate on a task, much as you can build lung capacity, then stamina, with aerobic exercise. The short answer to building up the ability to focus longer is to force yourself to stay with a task. So don't put down the puzzle the first time you hit a wall working it. Pause, if you like, to think a minute, but don't quit. If you are stuck, look at the hint printed upside down to get going again. Every time you don't quit you build the capacity to stick with it longer, if only a little. The effect is cumulative and worth the effort. If you can't concentrate you can't develop the *explicit* memory strategies you will need to enter new data into memory.

Beware of false memory. True memory can easily become distorted when you recall it. The brain organizes the vast store of data it must recall by piecing it back together in ways that follow other past experience. When details are missing, it tries to insert what "must" have happened. It will also fill in details that are suggested to it by the way a question is posed when you are asked to recall something.

Why you forget also reveals something about why you remember. When two bunches of data command your attention in sequence, such as when you read two stories in an anthology, your memory of details of the first will dim for a while, a natural occurrence called *retroactive inhibition*. That is why people sometimes find themselves in a place but can't recall what they went there for. Usually it is because something interesting commanded their attention on the way there.

That's Entertainment

DIRECTIONS

The answers to the clues are names. Choose a letter that appears at least once anywhere in the full name. The correct letter must appear as many times in the name as the available number of boxes allotted for each clue number, reading *across* only. (For example, 2 needs the first letters of her first and last names to fill its two boxes.) When correctly chosen, each row across will repeat the same letter. Each column will repeat the theme-word appropriate to this puzzle.

Didjaknow...

INFANTS FORGET WHEN DISTRACTED

An infant will reach for a reward placed under a cup, but if she sees you move it under another cup, and you distract her, she will look for it under the first cup. Because the brain has not matured enough to hold the new data, it only takes four seconds of diversion for the infant to forget the second action and revert to the first. Until language skills are acquired, the same forgetful response occurs in children two years of age or older when distraction is long-lasting between replacing the reward and reaching for it. For parents this can be a plus: next time your infant wants to grab a hazardous object, distract the infant by replacing the undesirable object with one that is safe.

Answer on page 108

1	2		3	
4				5
6			7	
8				9
10			11	

CLUES

1. Television and nightclub comedienne
2. Singer and movie actress
3. "Taxi" sit-com star
4. Hollywood's Butch Cassidy
5. New Orleans trumpeter
6. The "greatest" prizefighter
7. 1975 Wimbledon winner
8. Three baseball brothers
9. Early television comedian
10. Doyenne of the whodunit
11. Lucy's love

HINT: 5 is Al Hirt. Note that 8 includes the full names of all three brothers.

Birth of a Nation

DIRECTIONS

Solve this puzzle as you would a crossword puzzle using numbers instead of words. Only the digits 1 to 9 are used; there are no zeros. Only one digit may be placed in each box, and a digit may be used more than once in an answer. Where it appears that more than one combination of digits is possible, look for additional clues in the interlocking answers. A prime number is divisible only by itself and 1.

CLUES

ACROSS

1. The month and day of an American national holiday
3. A bad luck number
5. The year celebrated in 1 Across
7. A prime number, followed by its square and cube
8. The bicentennial anniversary of 5 Across
10. A good luck number

DOWN

2. The sum of its digits is 16
3. The first anniversary of 5 Across
4. A square
6. Well-known Boeing number plus 2
9. A square

Answer on page 108

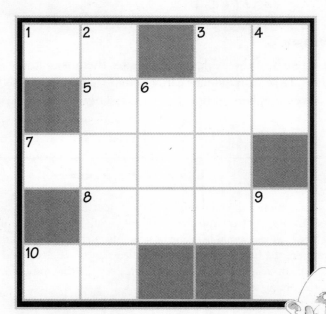

Didjaknow...   **WOMEN ARE BETTER AT VERBAL MEMORY**

In both immediate and delayed verbal memory, women outperform men. When asked to memorize a list of 16 items, most women knew the list on the second repetition, while it took men five tries. After a new "interference" list was given as a distraction, subjects were later asked to recite the first list. Again, women scored higher than the men on average.

HINT: Independence Day.

Digit-Tallies

DIRECTIONS

Next to each of the 20 letters, opposite, there is a group of seven numbers. How many groups can you find that are composed of the same seven numbers, although not necessarily in the same order?

Didjaknow...   EARLY TO BED MAKES YOU WISE

The student practice of cramming until dawn may lead to failure rather than success. Researchers find that, for most people, 6 to 8 hours of sleep is needed for optimal learning of new information. Particularly important are the first 2 hours of sleep, called slow-wave sleep, and the final 2 hours of sleep, called REM or dream sleep. During these sleep phases, the brain sorts, files, and stores data so it can be retrieved when needed. Students wanting to do well might want to close their books and head to bed early the night before an exam.

Answer on page 108

a	2 6 1 0 4 1 7
b	8 3 7 1 9 4 5
c	1 8 3 1 5 2 7
d	5 7 0 1 2 5 8
e	1 2 3 2 4 3 1
f	8 1 4 9 5 3 7
g	9 2 3 1 3 4 9
h	1 5 8 4 8 6 8
i	5 3 7 9 8 1 4
j	7 3 1 3 2 5 0

k	1 6 0 3 5 3 6
l	2 7 1 7 4 6 9
m	4 1 7 3 9 5 8
n	3 6 9 1 6 2 1
o	1 8 2 7 7 7 5
p	3 0 1 0 5 1 2
q	2 1 9 4 9 8 4
r	5 3 7 1 9 4 8
s	1 6 8 3 8 9 0
t	4 0 2 1 5 0 3

HINT: There are five groups with the same numbers.

Lucky Thirteen

DIRECTIONS

Your goal is to go from 13 to 181 in 10 moves, performing the arithmetical function to the digit in the square selected as you proceed. You may start from either corner but — and here's the trick — only one corner is correct. Moves may be made horizontally and vertically, but not diagonally.

Didjaknow...

YOUNG BRAINS AND OLD BRAINS DECLINE AT THE SAME RATE

Old brains DON'T decline more rapidly; they just begin to show it. A large sample of adults, between the ages of 20 to 90, underwent a battery of tests for working memory and overall mental function. The tests revealed how much information they could remember, manipulate, and retrieve. Interestingly, results revealed that brain decline begins when people are in their 20s and continues at the same pace across their entire lifespan.

Therefore, a 60- or 70-year-old brain is not actually declining any more rapidly than a 30-year-old's. Although the decline begins in young adulthood, the cumulative effects on brain function do not show up in behaviour until adults grow much older.

Answer on page 108

13	^{3} X	^{4} –	^{4} X	^{5} +	^{4} X	13
^{7} X	^{41} –	^{2} ÷	^{7} +	^{3} ÷	^{11} +	^{8} X
^{14} +	^{6} ÷	^{2} X	^{4} –	^{17} X	^{4} ÷	^{3} +
^{5} ÷	^{33} –	^{5} ÷	^{7} +	^{8} ÷	^{6} X	^{41} –
^{21} X	^{123} +	^{8} –	^{14} ÷	^{2} –	^{3} ÷	^{71} X
^{14} –	^{6} –	^{12} +	^{93} X	^{4} +	^{72} –	^{10} ÷
= 181	= 181	= 181	= 181	= 181	= 181	= 181

CITATIONS

P. 26 Diamond, Adele. "Learning and the Brain" Conference. Boston, MA, 7-9 Nov. 1999.

P. 29 Gur, Ruben C. PhD. Sex Differences in Learning. Using Brain Research to Reshape Classroom Practice. From a presentation at the Learning and the Brain Conference. Boston, Ma, 7-9 Nov. 1999.

P. 30 Stickgold, R. et al. (2000). Visual discrimination task improvement: a multi-step process occurring during sleep. Journal of Cognitive Neuroscience 12/2:246-54.

P. 32 Park, Denise PhD. The Center for Applied Cognitive Research on Aging, University of Michigan. From a presentation at the Science of Cognition Conference. Library of Congress, Washington, D.C., 6 Oct. 1999.

Section Three
COMPUTATION

What part of your brain will you be exercising as you work on the tasks in the Computation section? Many researchers believe there are different information-processing styles associated with each of your brain's hemispheres. The left is analytic, linear, serial-processing; it sees every tree in the forest, laboriously analysing and inspecting each in turn. The right is synthetic, simultaneous, parallel-processing; it quickly sizes up the shape and texture of the forest as a whole.

Language and maths may seem to be strictly linear, hence left-brain, skills. Both manipulate units of sound and sight (phonemes, syllables, digits and symbols) that can be combined in many ways according to rules. However, complex problem-solving skills like those must draw on systems in both hemispheres. For example, the flash of insight that led Einstein to his theory of relativity occurred as he considered the moving hands of the town-hall clock through the window of the moving tram on the way to work. That time-space insight was right-brain. The painstaking process of translating that insight into numbers was left-brain.

Two of the puzzle formats in this section are a lot like crossword puzzles with numbers rather than words. The interlocking answers to the clues help eliminate incorrect responses. The strategy is to fill in obvious answers as extra clues to pare down possibilities for the others. Take a look at the simplified fragment on the facing page, for example. If you look at each clue in turn, you'll see that every one suggests multiple solutions. Any line of boxes, taken alone, could be filled in with any of several answers, but only some of those answers could be compatible with the clues given for intersecting lines of boxes.

Clues:

1 Across	13 x 1, 2, or 3
3 Across	A palindrome; the first digit is the square root of the last two
2 Down	A square

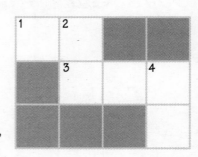

For example, 1 Across could be 13, 26, or 39 and 2 Down could be 16, 25, 36, 49, 64, or 81. But since the second digit of 1 Across is also the first digit of 2 Down, the latter could only be 36 or 64.

So 3 Across must begin with 6 or 4. Let's say it begins with 6. Since the answer must be a palindrome (a number that reads the same forwards and backwards), and the first digit must be the square root of the last two, the answer could be 636. What about the other possibility? If 3 Across begins with 4, then the next two digits would have to be 16 by the square root requirement — but then, it wouldn't be a palindrome. So 3 Across must be 636, 2 Down must be 36, 1 Across must be 13.

To review a few terms: A "square" of any number (say 3) is the number you get when you multiply it by itself (9). The "square root" is the number you started with (3). A "cube" results from multiplying that answer again by itself (81). A "prime" number is any one that cannot be divided evenly except by 1 and itself (For example, 3 or 7 are , but not 6 or 21). "Digits" are the basic numbers in a system or set. In our decimal system they are 0 through 10; in binary system code they are 0 and 1. "Integers" are the numbers you say when you count. Have fun!

Oops, Sorry, Dick!

Last month when Dick had to do jury duty, Tom volunteered to prepare the invoices based on their hardware store's receipts. He had just one invoice left to do when the electric adding machine suddenly went silent and he was left to his own devices. With a slight shrug of the shoulders, Tom calculated the cost of each item and mailed out the statement shown below. A few days later he received a visit from an irate customer waving his copies of the sales slips. Dick was back from jury duty and saw immediately what Tom had done wrong. All the digits in the cost of each item were either one digit higher or one digit lower than they should have been. For example, Tom wrote down an 8 when he should have written a 7 or 9. In fact, Tom wrote only one of the digits correctly, and that was in the price for the spotlight.

INVOICE	
Trolley jack	£218.49
Vice	26.81
Spotlight	25.59
	£270.89

Answer on page 109

Dick corrected the invoice and the total came to £170 exactly, which saved the customer a little over £100. Can you calculate the correct cost of each of the three items so they total £170?

Didjaknow... **SOCIAL FACTORS INFLUENCE MENTAL DISORDERS**

Physical and mental health is influenced by our social environment and life experience. A life of "hard times" often causes an early decline in physical health, mental health, and abilities, including computational skills. Those at the low end of the scale, socially and economically, seem to have more problems with certain mental disorders, such as seasonal affective disorder (the "winter blues"), anxiety disorder, and substance abuse. Social and environmental factors such as low birth weight, lack of parental support, abuse and neglect, all influence the development of mental illness and disorders. However, vulnerability also depends on an individual's choices, lifestyle, access to information, and feeling of self-worth.

HINT: Since each digit can be replaced by only another single digit, the nines, if they are only one digit too low, become zeros.

Wall To Wall Bags

Tom and Dick, hardware dealers extraordinaire, also have a Boy Scout troop. When school was over for the summer they took the troop of 32 boys up to the mountains for a few days camping. The shelter was a single large room with space for exactly 14 sleeping bags along each of the four walls. Tom assigned spaces as shown opposite (A). When Dick pointed out that they and the two fathers who were driving would need space

for their sleeping bags as well, he suggested an alternate plan (B).

Then it was remembered that four Boy Scouts had brought along younger brothers who had paid their own way, and the room plan was changed again to accommodate them (C).

All went well until the last night of camping. Four leaders who had been taking a refresher course in wilderness survival asked for shelter from a heavy rainstorm. Again the sleeping bags were moved (D).

At all times the limitation of 14 bags along each wall was met. How did they manage it?

Answer on page 109

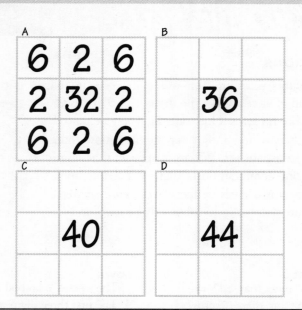

A
6	2	6
2	32	2
6	2	6

B
	36	

C
	40	

D
	44	

Didjaknow... BODY AND BRAIN DIFFERENTIATE STRESS

Stressful life events affect the health of the body and the brain. However, there is a difference between generally "feeling stressed out" and real stress. The sympathetic nervous system includes the adrenal glands which produce both adrenaline and cortisol. The autonomic nervous system produces catecholamines and regulates the production of cortisol. Stress such as physical activity, a state of arousal, and fear stimulate adrenaline production. Cortisol production increases in times of more pronounced stress, such as a severe change or threat to one's life, particularly when it is related to an unexpected event and strongly-felt emotions.

HINT: The corner numbers in B are 5

Counter Intelligence

DIRECTIONS

Solve this puzzle as you would a crossword puzzle using numbers instead of words. Only the digits 1 to 9 are used; there are no zeros. Only one digit may be placed in each box, and a digit may be used more than once in an answer. Where it appears that more than one combination of digits is possible, look for additional clues in the interlocking answers. A prime number is divisible only by itself and 1.

CLUES

ACROSS

1. Two more than 8 Down
3. Ten more than 1 Across
5. The first day of winter
7. The seventh day of the Jewish festival of Chanukah
8. Christmas Day
10. The square of an even number that itself is a cube
11. A multiple of 1 Across

DOWN

2. The square of an odd number
3. The first three digits are alike, so are the last two
4. The sum of the first two digits is equal to the third
6. Boiling point
8. The square of an even number
9. The second digit is double the first

Answer on page 109

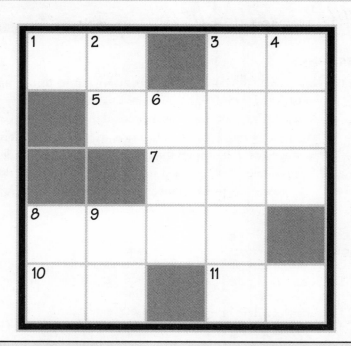

Didjaknow... **EINSTEIN'S SPECIAL GENIUS WAS RIGHT-BRAINED**

The great physicist was not a genius at maths. In school, he struggled with left-brain learning: computation and language skills (reading, writing and spelling). He did not learn to speak until age three. All his life, most of his thinking was without words. His extraordinary right brain abilities equipped him to visualize concepts into space-time configurations. He laboured to translate his insights into mathematics.

HINT: 7 Across is 129

Figuratively Speaking

DIRECTIONS

Solve this puzzle as you would a crossword puzzle using numbers instead of words. Only the digits 1 to 9 are used; there are no zeros. Only one digit may be placed in each box, and a digit may be used more than once in an answer. Where it appears that more than one combination of digits is possible, look for additional clues in the interlocking answers. A prime number is divisible only by itself and 1.

CLUES

ACROSS

1. Consecutive digits, all odd
5. The symmetrical cube of a digit in 1 Across
6. The square of a digit in 1 Across; the sum of its digits equals the root
7. The square of a digit in 1 Across
8. The symmetrical square of a prime number
10. Consecutive digits

DOWN

2. The sum of the first two digits is equal to the sum of the last three
3. Consecutive digits
4. The sum of the last three digits equals the product of the first two
9. The cube of a digit in 1 Across

Answer on page 109

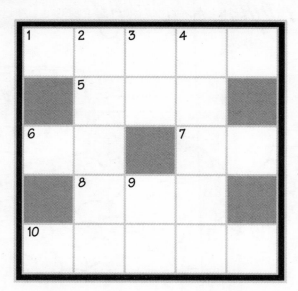

Didjaknow... TESTOSTERONE DECLINE LEADS TO SOME LOSS OF MATHS SKILLS

Men tend to be better at maths than women, but both will show decline in mathematical ability with age. Brain studies of men show that the hippocampus, a structure that processes mathematical and spatial problems, shrinks more rapidly in men and is directly affected by declining testosterone levels. Since testosterone levels are highest in young adult males, this explains why most maths prodigies are males and why these prodigies reach top expertise in their 20s, then decline in ability thereafter.

HINT: *Begin with 5 and 8 Across, then 9 Down.*

Not Apples & Oranges

A greengrocer, whose organic produce market was stocked with good intentions but was losing money, complained to his suppliers that oranges were selling well at 45 p a pound (a fair price), but no one was buying his grapefruit at 60 p a pound. Tom suggested that the greengrocer combine the two fruits, bagging them proportionately, and selling them at 50 p a pound. The greengrocer weighed 20 pounds of grapefruit but had no idea how many oranges would be required. But his supplier, eager to sell his grapefruit, came up with the answer. Can you do this one in your head?

Answer on page 109

Didjaknow...

GAZING TO THE RIGHT STIMULATES MATHS SKILLS

Do you dread having to fill out and file tax forms? Do you put off the monthly act of balancing your cheque book because tasks involving numbers leave you yawning? Next time you have to perform a chore that involves mathematical computation, try placing a plant, picture or cherished item to the right side of your viewing field and glance at it every so often. Researchers say looking to the right stimulates left-brain maths skills and should make the process of mathematics flow easier. Go figure — and gaze to the right.

HINT: Use "n" for the required number of pounds. That number times the cost per pound equals the selling price.

Summing Up

DIRECTIONS

Solve this puzzle as you would a crossword puzzle, using interlocking numbers instead of words. Write a single digit in each box so that the sum of the digits equals the total given for that row or column in the Across and Down clues. For example, the sum of the digits in the 1-Across boxes must total 34. No number is used more than once in any answer, and zero is not used. The digits already in place are correct.

CLUES

ACROSS

1. 34	12. 28
5. 17	14. 24
6. 11	17. 20
8. 30	18. 33
10. 16	
11. 15	

DOWN

1. 28	9. 20
2. 21	11. 28
3. 10	13. 24
4. 17	15. 11
5. 32	16. 13
7. 31	

Didjaknow... COUNTING AND QUANTITY ARE TWO DIFFERENT CONCEPTS

Even though your child may be able to count to 10, this does not mean he understands that the number-word represents a quantity. Stack 9 blocks and ask your youngster to count them. Next, point to the stack and ask him how many blocks you placed in the stack. If he has to count again, he does not yet grasp the concept that the last number counted in a sequence signifies the quantity of the whole set.

Answer on page 109

	1	2	**7**	3	4	
5				6		7
8			9			**6**
10			**7**		11	
8			12	13		
14	15	16		17		
	18		**7**			

Add-Vance Notice

DIRECTIONS

Solve this puzzle as you would a crossword puzzle, using interlocking numbers instead of words. Write a single digit in each box so that the sum of the digits equals the total given for that row or column in the Across and Down clues. For example, the sum of the digits in the 1-Across boxes must total 18. No number is used more than once in any answer, and zero is not used. We have entered some correct digits as checkpoints.

CLUES

ACROSS		DOWN	
1. 18	15. 20	1. 25	11. 33
3. 19	16. 30	2. 15	15. 26
7. 13	18. 17	4. 13	17. 23
9. 22	19. 24	5. 27	20. 15
11. 13	21. 12	6. 13	22. 14
12. 28	24. 27	8. 34	23. 16
13. 25	25. 24	9. 32	
14. 20		10. 35	

Answer on page 109

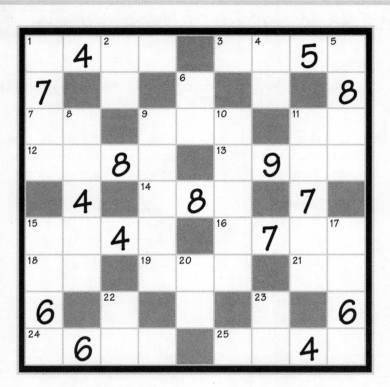

Didjaknow... A MYSTERIOUS AFFINITY FOR 7S

The brain seems to put a limit on remembering a sequence of numbers at seven digits. Many systems are based on this limitation; days in the week, telephone numbers, and notes on the musical scale, for example.

HINT: 1 and 2 are not used.

Adds & Evens

DIRECTIONS

Solve this puzzle as you would a crossword puzzle, using interlocking numbers instead of words. Write a single digit in each box so that the sum of the digits equals the total given for that row or column in the Across and Down clues. For example, the sum of the digits in the 1-Across boxes must total 18. No number is used more than once in any answer, and zero is not used. The entered digits are correct.

CLUES

ACROSS
1. 18
4. 8
7. 11
8. 22
9. 17
10. 23
12. 12
13. 39
16. 26
17. 26
19. 21
21. 14
23. 17
25. 13
26. 22
27. 11
28. 18
29. 21

DOWN
1. 18
2. 35
3. 23
5. 16
6. 29
11. 24
12. 20
14. 13
15. 21
16. 35
18. 35
20. 22
22. 18
24. 18

Didjaknow...   JAPANESE WORDS FOR NUMBERS HELP THEM LEARN MATHS EARLY

The Japanese learn to count earlier than English-speaking children, in part, because the names for numbers between 10 and 100 represent the numbers 1 through 9. For example, the number 10 is named "zyuu" and the number 2 is named "ni." The number-name for 12 is "zyuuni" or 10 + 2. Besides assisting with counting skills, the Japanese number-name system teaches the concept of quantity, making addition easier to grasp.

Answer on page 109

1	2			3		4	5	6
7			8	5			9	
10		11				12		
	13		14		15			
16	6				17		18	
		19		20				
21	22			4		23		24
25			26				27	
28						29		

HINT: All the numbers in rows and columns end with even digits.

CITATIONS

P. 39, 40 McEwen, Bruce PhD., Head of the Hatch Laboratory of
Neuroendocrinology, Rockefeller University. From a presentation at the Science
of Cognition Conference, Library of Congress, Washington, D.C., 6 Oct. 1999.

P. 42, 44, 48, 50, 52 Bragdon, A., Gamon, D. (2001) The Brainwaves Center, Bass
River, MA.

P. 46 Kinsbourne, M. (1983). Lateral input may shift activation balance in the
integrated brain. Psychologist 38:228-9.
Levick, S.E. et al. (1993). Asymmetrical visual deprivation: a technique to
differentially influence lateral hemispheric function. Perceptual Motor Skills
76:1363-82.

Section Four
SPATIAL

Visuospatial *scratchpad* is the term neuroscientists use to refer to a Working Memory tool you will be using when you tackle tasks like the mental exercises on the following pages. Some of the exercises require you to visualize forms in space as architects, builders, sculptors and chess masters must do. In everyday life people use this skill to, for example, fit suitcases into a car's boot or find their way back to the entrance of a building or relocate their car in a shopping centre parking lot.

The right hemisphere of most male brains is more highly specialized for that kind of skill than the female brain normally is. This is one of the most obvious gender differences in cognitive processing and it seems to correlate with what is known about how protohuman primates lived when their brains were evolving 60 million years ago. Women find their way by identifying landmarks. Men are more likely to orient themselves to large geographical reference points, including the sun and stars. It is tempting to speculate that, as hunters, males travelled long distances drawn by game into unfamiliar territory. Women, who kept close to their dwelling to care for infants and to escape predators, would have been more likely to rely on local landmarks to move around seeking food or firewood in familiar territory near their dwelling.

The visuospatial skills can be developed with practice. A recent neuroscientific study of experienced, professional taxi drivers in London, who are required to pass rigorous tests in finding addresses anywhere in the city before they are licensed, showed that a portion of their brain was significantly larger than that of London workers in other jobs. It is called the *hippocampus*, based on the latin word for horse, (as hippopotamus also is), because at one time somebody must have thought that organ and animal each looked like a horse, (which they don't at all). Every brain has one on each side. The one on the right side, where visuospatial skills are located for most people, was larger in the London cabbies' brains. The neurons in the rear part of that area had sent out more connections to respond to the daily performance demanded of them. This forced an increase in mass which is clearly noticeable in a brain scan.

That finding is a persuasive example of a fact that is little known but is very encouraging. The human brain is able to adapt physically to meet demands put to it, much as a society can change its values in a common crisis or a flower will grow toward the sun's light. This means that the brain responds as other physical systems do. Aerobic exercise builds strength in the heart muscle and oxygen-carrying capacity in the lungs, thereby increasing stamina. Muscle groups gain mass when they are subjected to the regular stresses of targeted exercises. Lifting and running capacity increase as a result. Even if a system has not been used for many years, its mass and effectiveness can be revived with exercise which, incidentally, shows up dramatically in older people who start exercising after leading relatively sedentary lives.

Like life, there is a downside. In the Middle Ages the crafts of architecture, building and draughtsmanship — all trades that target the visuospatial centers in the right hemisphere — were known as the melancholy arts because they were thought to depress the spirit. In fact, the right hemisphere does process negative facial expressions and is more active in the depressed phase of a manic-depressive cycle. But that didn't stop Leonardo da Vinci, nor should it you.

A Piece of Cake

DIRECTIONS

Six hungry boys "borrowed" a chocolate cake from one of their mothers and took it to their secret clubhouse to divide up. But their felonious act had been witnessed by a younger sister and her friend who offered to be silent on the matter in return for a piece of cake each. The boys agreed but set a condition: they would take their pieces first and the girls must select the seventh and eighth pieces in the order the boys had established when they took the first six pieces. The girls quickly saw the pattern and chose the correct seventh piece. Can you?

Didjaknow... SUPERIOR MALE SPATIAL SKILLS MAY BE EVOLUTIONARY

Men are better than women at spatial tasks that involve orientation and navigational skill. This makes sense if you look at evolution, gender role, and survival of our species. During the pre-agricultural hunter-gatherer era, men were primarily hunters and these navigational abilities would be necessary for traveling and tracking game. Women, on the other hand, remained close to home, nursing and tending children.

Answer on page 110

An "L" of a Time

DIRECTIONS

Tom has always been interested in the electric tools he and his brother Dick carry in their hardware store. On one slow day recently he took out a piece of graph paper and began planning a layout for a parquet counter-top insert. It would be composed of eight L-shaped pieces of veneer fitted together to form a square, but after several attempts he was ready to give up. Dick watched for a while, then suggested cutting four L shapes and four Z shapes. Do you know how these can be arranged to form a square.

Didjaknow...

CARICATURES SUBTRACT AND AMPLIFY

When a rat is rewarded for responding to a rectangle instead of a square, the rat's response to a longer and narrower rectangle is even greater, due to a cognitive principle called the "peak-shift" effect. Artists rely on the same cognitive rule when they produce caricature art. When a cartoonist draws a caricature of a famous face, such as Gordon Brown, the artist visualizes the average of all faces and subtracts that from Brown's face. By rendering the differences, the finished drawing exaggerates features, creating a sketch that looks more like Gordon Brown than Gordon Brown himself.

Answer on page 110

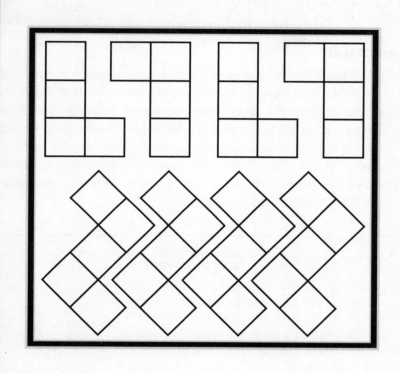

Crunchy Cake

DIRECTIONS

When you celebrate a birthday in the land of Klunk, it is customary to embed coins of various denominations rather than candles in the icing of the birthday cake. Moreover, the guest of honour must cut the cake in such a way that the coins amount to the same total in every piece. Of course, this usually results in some very peculiar-looking pieces of cake. If it were your birthday and you had six guests, how would you cut the cake so the coins in all seven pieces would equal the same total?

Didjaknow... BRAIN ENJOYS VISUAL BINDING AND DISCOVERY TASKS

For survival, vision evolved so an individual is able to discern camouflaged objects. In order to do this, the brain has to assemble partially-hidden pieces of visual data into a recognizable object. For example, if we view a coyote behind green shrubbery, our visual brain links all the grey areas, combining them together to create the coyote's image. The very nature of this task seems to be a pleasing one: scientists indicate this binding and discovery process creates a positive emotional response, possibly by sending signals directly to our limbic brain where emotions originate.

Answer on page 110

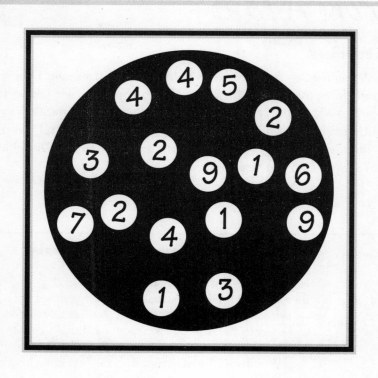

From A to B

DIRECTIONS

All you have to do to solve this puzzle is move in a single, unbroken path from the upper right corner (a) to the lower left corner (b). But, to add a little interest to the problem, your path must take you alternately through square, circle, square, circle, etc. And you may not move diagonally — only vertically and horizontally. We did it in 27 moves. Can you beat that?

Didjaknow... TESTOSTERONE AFFECTS SPATIAL ABILITY

Men are generally better than women at tasks that involve spatial ability. Test results prove that males outperform females on tasks that involve mental rotations of 3-dimensional objects. The reason for this is apparently gender-based and hormonal. Studies were done on infants who were born with the correct male chromosomes (X and Y), yet lacked receptors for the male hormone testosterone. Later in life, school tests showed these males scored lower than "normal" males on tests involving spatial and mathematical skills.

Answer on page 110

Assyrian Miss-tery

DIRECTIONS

Shortly after the artist made this rendering of an ancient Assyrian bas relief, ten pieces mysteriously disappeared. They were recently found in a basement in Bismarck, North Dakota, and put back in their correct positions. The small squares above and below the drawing show the missing pieces. Can you find which sections they belong to? When you locate them, place their letters and numbers in the boxes next to each square. One has already been identified to show how it's done.

Didjaknow... TRANSSEXUALS HAVE BRAIN CHANGE

Sex differences in brain function are due to hormonal influence according to a study done by researchers in the Netherlands. Transsexuals showed the same sex differences in brain function as a biological-born gender. When transsexuals were studied, males that were changed into females declined on spatial ability but improved on verbal functioning. On immediate and delayed memory performance testing, these "new" females tested better than males. Vice versa, females changed to the male gender showed improved spatial ability but declined on verbal fluency. Sex hormones are the only explanation for this phenomenon.

Answer on page 110

CITATIONS

P. 58 Bragdon, Allen D. The Brainwaves Center, Bass River, MA (2001).

P. 60, 62 Ramachandran, V.S. MD, PhD. Professor and Director, Center for Brain and Cognition, University of California-San Diego. From a presentation at the Science of Cognition Conference. Library of Congress. Washington, D. C., 6 Oct. 1999.

P. 64 Bragdon, Allen and Gamon, David PhD. "Building Left Brain Power," Brainwaves Books, Bass River, MA (2000).

P. 66 Gur, Ruben C. Sex Differences in Learning. Using Brain Research to Reshape Classroom Practice. Public Information Resources, Inc. 7-9 Nov. 1999.

Section Five
LANGUAGE

Have you heard about the latest brain research? If you stimulate your brain with cognitive challenges, you'll raise its dopamine levels. Dopamine is a neurotransmitter produced by the brain to facilitate passing signals among brain cells. Dopamine also makes you feel good by causing a rewarding sense of satisfaction, especially when the brain works on a left-hemisphere task like a word task. The same stimulus-reward system is activated by some narcotics. Your brain loves to feel good. If it can't do it by solving puzzles, it'll look for other means. The puzzles are generally better for you than the other means that don't add to your vocabulary much.

Consider, just for a moment, how lucky we humans are to be able to learn our language all by ourselves at such an early age that we think life is *supposed* to be that much work. Infants and young children learn the basic structure, pronunciation, grammar and most of the vocabulary of their native language independently of the teaching skills of their parents. Self-education in acquisition of a skill that complex is a stroke of brilliance in brain design. Recruiting a self-motivating neurotransmitter like dopamine as a player in that process is a second masterstroke. Together, they seem to verify that brain design, like the design of a lasting political constitution, requires a realistic appraisal of human motivations and self-interest.

English is trickier than most languages. It is harder to read, write, and spell English words, and make sense of fast-moving conversation and printed paragraphs. The incidence of dyslexia, for example, is lower in non-English-speaking communities. The difference is not schooling, it is the consistency of the language.

The 40-odd sounds in English can be written in over 1000 different ways. The brain has to work faster to decode English sentences — does that "gh" sound like the "ff" in tough or the "gas" in ghastly, or what? In Italian, for example, you get just what you see, every time. The fact that Italy has half as many dyslexic children per capita as the United States may be because the human brain can decode the sounds of an Italian sentence milliseconds faster than the same sentence in English. Milliseconds count in processing word comprehension of a new language — a child in preschool could tell you that (as soon as he learns to speak his native tongue, of course).

What part of your brain will you be exercising in this section of the book? Left, mostly. The right side is more active in Sections 4 and 6. Word processing may seem exclusively left-brain linear because you must keep track of sound- and meaning-units produced in rapid sequence. Some aspects of language recall are linear, but not all. You can't "get" verbal jokes or puns unless you hold multiple ideas in your head at once — an ability shared by the front part of both hemispheres, but mostly the right. Incidentally, the burst of laughter that follows a good joke also enlists circuits of stimulus and reward. The stimulus is to search for how the surprising punch line *does* follow the set-up story line. When the punch-line hits, your brain relishes scurrying around to figure out how the unexpected fits. The reward part comes when you "get" it.

We designed these exercises to help you feel good and stay smart. Few other things in life that are so good for you are this much fun.

Bizarre Route

DIRECTIONS

Rearrange each group of letters to form a different word, then place the new words in the grid, starting each in its numbered square, so that each word reads the same across and down, e.g., 1 Across and 1 Down read the same, 2 Across and 2 Down read the same, etc. Clues to the correct words for three of the groups are given in parentheses.

Didjaknow... WRITING TEST REVEALS LEFT-HANDED THINKING

Although most left-handers process language in the right hemisphere of their brains, this is not true for all lefties. If you are left handed, a team of scientists say a simple writing test can reveal which side of the brain controls your language skills: if you write with your left hand *below* the line of writing, as right-handers do, your dominant language hemisphere is opposite from your writing hand (therefore right); if you write with your hand in a hooked position *above* the line, then your left brain is processing language as it normally does for right-handed people.

Answer on page 111

1	2	3	4	5
2				
3				
4				
5				

CLUES

1. CHUCO (sofa)
2. ROUTE (extreme, Fr.)
3. TRUET
4. ECERD
5. DERSH (groups)

HINT: *The answer to 4 is* CREED.

Thoughtful Browsing

DIRECTIONS

To find the words to an old adage, start with the top word in each column and change one letter as you go down the ladder. The dot in the box shows which letter needs to be changed. Letters do not change position with any move. The Mystery Words at the bottom of the ladders, when solved and unscrambled, will form a well-known saying. Cognitive Chick is holding an extra Mystery Word that is used in the saying, and she has started one ladder to get you going.

Didjaknow... LEARNING DISABILITIES CAN OFTEN BE OUTGROWN

Parents and teachers often see children who do not fit common definitions of learning disabilities. Like faces, our brains differ in arrangement and proportion. Some children with learning disabilities actually have brain anomalies which, in certain cases, can actually be outgrown. When a child shows symptoms of abnormal behaviour, such as poor language skill, it could be due to brain areas that are not fully developed or are developing abnormally. In a young person, new circuits may be able to replace the abnormal ones and language skills will eventually be mastered. However, if all the language centres have fully matured and the disability has not been overcome, the deficit is likely to be permanent.

Answer on page 111

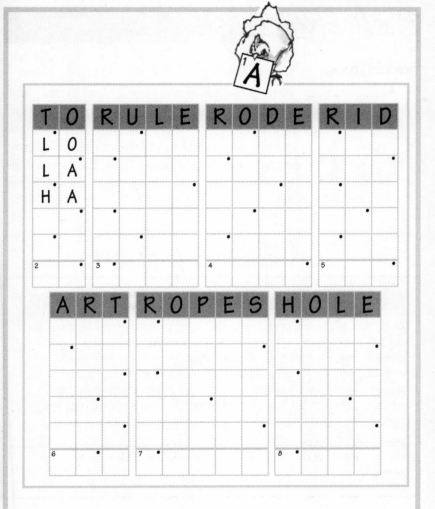

T	O
L	O
L	A
H	A
2	

R	U	L	E
3			

R	O	D	E
4			

R	I	D
5		

A	R	T
6		

R	O	P	E	S
7				

H	O	L	E
8			

HINT: The answer to Mystery Word 5 is YOU.

Bah Humbug!

DIRECTIONS

Arguments begin when one word leads to another, and in this puzzle words not only lead to each other, but often overlap. If you start in slot #1 with the right word and continue clockwise you should have little trouble completing the circle with 14 additional words. Each word starts in a numbered slot that corresponds to the number of the clue.

Didjaknow... FEMALE BRAIN MORE LIKELY TO USE BOTH SIDES FOR LANGUAGE

Until recently, scientists thought that most people process language in the left hemisphere of the brain. Now researchers know this generalization is more valid for men than for women. Apparently, women's verbal processing areas are more likely to be distributed throughout both sides of the brain. Female patients with injury or strokes to the left hemisphere of the brain show fewer language deficits than males and are better able to recover language skills.

Answer on page 111

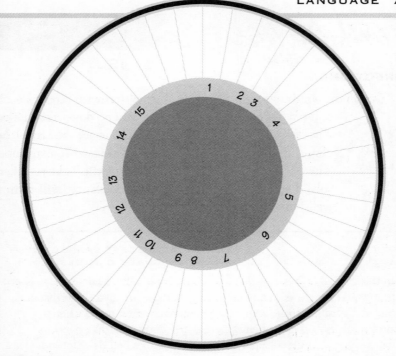

CLUES

1. Audio distortion
2. ___ of the cloth (ecclesiastic)
3. South American mountain range
4. Fate
5. Lesser goddess
6. Irrational fear
7. Prejudice
8. Inquire
9. Pervert; distort
10. Ram's mate
11. Existed once
12. Take up again
13. Staircase post
14. Mischievous
15. Complete

HINT: 6 is PHOBIA

Fowl Advice

DIRECTIONS

To find the words to a wise old adage, start with the top word in each column and change one letter as you go down the ladder. The dot in the box shows which letter needs to be changed. Letters do not change position with any move. The Mystery Words at the bottom of the ladders, when solved and arranged in the correct sequence, will form a well-known saying.

Didjaknow... STROKES IN THE LEFT BRAIN OFTEN DAMAGE LANGUAGE CENTRES

In the United States over half a million people suffer brain damage from strokes each year and one-quarter of those are fatal. Disturbances in speech and language comprehension are often observed when a stroke occurs in the left hemisphere of the brain. A stroke happens when the brain's blood supply is blocked due to a break or clot in a blood vessel. Brain cells that are deprived of oxygen die within minutes, releasing certain chemicals that trigger a chain reaction that is harmful to surrounding brain tissue. Language-processing cells that are only stunned, not killed, often regain their function in time. In younger people, especially, other parts of the brain will take over language speaking or comprehension tasks from damaged areas where those functions are normally processed.

Answer on page 111

Bespoke in Spokane

DIRECTIONS

Arguments begin when one word leads to another, and in this puzzle words not only lead to each other, but often overlap. If you start in slot 1 with the right word and continue clockwise you should have little trouble completing the circle with 17 additional words. Each word starts in a numbered slot that corresponds to the number of the clue.

CLUES

1. Wheel part
2. Understanding
3. Stage direction
4. Dist.
5. Off course
6. Rave's partner
7. Part of the pot
8. Try
9. High regard
10. Swarm
11. Blend; participate
12. Faint light
13. Saunter
14. Rent
15. Delineate sharply
16. Dear in France
17. Thyme, e.g.
18. Engaged to be married

Didjaknow... TWO CODES ARE BETTER THAN ONE

Memory can be divided into three temporal stages. In the first , the encoding stage, information (visual and/or verbal) is presented. During the second stage, information is stored and frequently reinforced. The third, or retrieval, stage occurs when stored information is remembered.

Answer on page 111

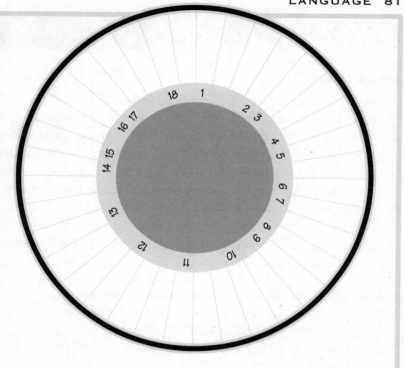

You are more likely to remember an object if you are shown a picture of it, rather than just hearing the word that names the object. For example, when you see a picture of an object such as a lizard, you are encoding visual information plus the name "lizard". If you are asked to remember the object later, the visual and verbal codes combine to give you a better memory than one single code of just a simple word.

HINT: 11 is MINGLE.

Colourful Conundrum

DIRECTIONS

Start at a single letter (A, I, or E) and add two letters to it to spell a three-letter word in the next row. Continue until you complete the colourful (or colourless) Mystery Word at the end of the ladder. You may rearrange the letters to spell each new word. Work the centre puzzle from the single letter I to the top, and the other two, from A and E, to the bottom. No proper nouns, abbreviated, hyphenated, or foreign words are allowed. Each letter falling in a circle is worth the number of points shown in the "letter values" column on the opposite page. Try to complete words that offer the highest score.

Didjaknow... DYSLEXIA MAY BE A PHONOLOGICAL PROBLEM

By asking a child to translate words into Pig Latin, scientists can measure the ability to identify sounds in words. This phonological test requires recognizing the first sound of a word, moving it to the end of the word, and adding an additional sound. To achieve this task, a child must be able to remember the word substructure ready for manipulation, just as he must remember sounds while sounding out a new word. When attempting this task, dyslexic children take significantly longer and make more errors than children with good reading skills. While attempting to read, some dyslexic children not only report visual complaints, such as "the words seem to be moving," but many also experience and report difficulties linking a written syllable with its sound.

Answer on page 11·1

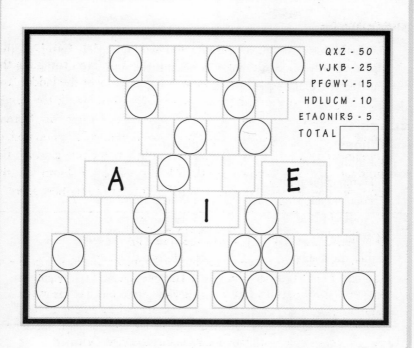

QXZ - 50
VJKB - 25
PFGWY - 15
HDLUCM - 10
ETAONIRS - 5
TOTAL

A   E
      I

Ditch That Truck!

DIRECTIONS

In this crossword puzzle format, you will use each letter of the alphabet only once. To make things a little more interesting, we've omitted the black squares.

CLUES

ACROSS

3. Kipling poem
4. Disreputable joint
6. Popular gait
8. An R of R&R
10. Wildcat
11. Electrical abbr.

DOWN

1. ___ code
2. "_____ the Raven…"
4. Music MCs
5. British sports car
7. _____ Hills, Dakota
8. MD's asst.
9. Former
12. Foreign car mfr.

Didjaknow... LEFT BRAIN USUALLY LEARNS LANGUAGE

Researchers think that language is generally processed in the left hemisphere of the brain because during infancy the right hemisphere is busy processing early, less complicated information. As an infant matures and cognition increases, the left hemisphere is accessible and ready to take on the detailed and specialized processing that language learning involves.

Answer on page 112

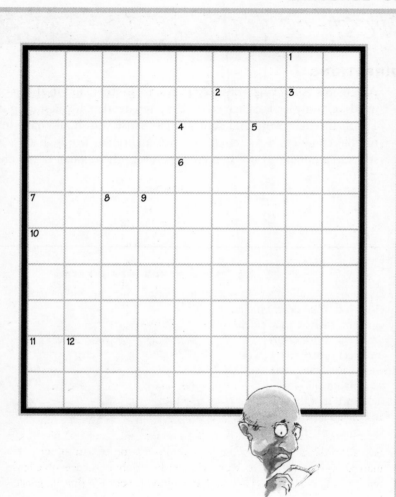

N'est-ce Pas?

DIRECTIONS

Arguments begin when one word leads to another, and in this puzzle words not only lead to each other, but often overlap. If you start in slot 1 with the right word and continue clockwise you should have little trouble completing the circle with 16 additional words. Each word starts in a numbered slot that corresponds to the number of the clue.

Didjaknow... FALSE WORDS IMPAIR FACTS

Language is a valuable tool for communication, thought, and memory. However, when describing an object or event, such as an accident or a car, if the words create incorrect descriptive values and images, they can actually impair later recognition of the actual car and create false beliefs of the factual event. This happens because an inaccurate verbal description can often override a more precise nonverbal memory.

Answer on page 112

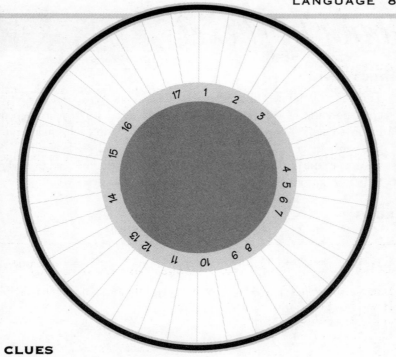

CLUES

1. ___ egg (retirement fund perhaps)
2. Baby bird
3. Scottish islands
4. Ogle
5. Affirmative
6. City in NE Italy
7. Vapour
8. Etiquette's Vanderbilt
9. Talking bird
10. Kind of tag
11. Nourishing occasion
12. Mohammed ___
13. Schulz character
14. More than often
15. Bedfellow
16. Kind of poem
17. Flog

HINT: 9 is MYNA.

Hang In There!

DIRECTIONS

This puzzle combines anagrams and word hunts. Write out the letters corresponding to the numbers (A=1, B=2, etc.), then rearrange the letters to make a new word that fits the clue. Fill in each square in the grid with its corresponding number and find and circle each of the answers in the grid. Some words are diagonal, and some read from right to left or bottom to top. The first definition is done for you.

CLUES

A. 1 12 7 12 15 23 19 — Capone shines scaffold
AL GLOWS/GALLOWS

B. 7 18 1 9 12 13 15 20 8 — Insect on knightly quest finds mathematical exponent

C. 14 5 1 20 13 1 9 4 — Tidy hired help was lively

D. 12 5 1 4 — Metal for trade

E. 20 18 1 9 20 — Characteristic of singer John

F. 1 23 18 25 — Wrong to be cautious

G. 4 21 14 5 19 — Sahara sights uncovered objects

H. 20 9 5 7 1 12 — Even girl can use a bandage

I. 4 21 1 12 — Twofold praise

J. 18 5 1 12 12 19 20 — Sincere Navy craft is starlike

K. 19 5 1 18 20 15 5 — Optimistic after hot foot

L. 13 15 18 5 22 9 16 — Sir Thomas Big Shot will get better

M. 19 5 14 19 9 20 9 22 5 — Touchy when social call was sighted (two words)

N. 20 1 13 5 4 18 15 3 — Subdued fabulous bird and formed military group (two words)

14	5	5	19	20	9	19	9	22	14
19	20	5	12	12	1	18	4	5	13
20	1	5	2	20	18	5	1	8	14
15	5	20	23	21	20	18	20	19	21
4	19	1	4	1	16	9	14	5	4
5	15	7	13	21	18	7	1	1	5
22	18	9	2	1	1	25	5	18	19
18	14	12	7 *G*	1 *A*	12 *L*	12 *L*	15 *O*	23 *W*	19 *S*
1	9	15	5	22	15	18	16	13	9
3	12	13	1	14	5	18	15	20	3

O. 18 5 16 21 2 12 9 3 1 14   Elephantine politico close by the community at large (two words)

P. 9 14 4 5 16   ____endence Day languished?

Q. 13 5 4   Resort club becomes abbreviated party

R. 3 1 22 15 18 20 5 4   Leaped about first, then slice Dorothy (two words)

S. 25 5 1   Indeed yes!

HINT: E is RAITT

CITATIONS:

P. 72, 84, 70, 86 (2001) The Brainwaves Center, Bass River, MA.

P. 74 Denckla, Martha Bridge, MD, Director, Developmental Cognitive Neurology, The John Hopkins School of Medicine. From a Presentation at Science of Cognition Conference, Library of Congress, Washington, D.C., 6 Oct. 1999.

P. 78 American Stroke Association (2000).

P. 80 Petersen, Steven E. PhD., Professor, Department of Neurology and Neurological Surgery, Washington University School of Medicine. From a presentation at Science of Cognition Conference, Library of Congress, Washington, D.C., 6 Oct. 1999.

P. 82 Eden, Guinevere D. Phil., Georgetown University Medical Center. From a presentation at the Science of Cognition Conference, Library of Congress, Washington, D.C., 6 Oct. 1999.

Section Six
SOCIAL-EMOTIONAL

Consciousness in humans is awareness of emotions. Emotions are the exposed tips of responses to sub-conscious survival-needs that our primitive brain systems pick up — immediate danger, opportunities to reproduce, sources of food. Humans can become consciously aware of some of their body's automatic reactions set in motion by unconscious responses to basic survival stimuli. The human animal may be unique in its ability to see itself as a player in the primitive drama of survival. It can then control its emotional reactions, sometimes, with an eye to future benefit. In his book "The Feeling of What Happens", Antonio R. Damasio calls that self-awareness "consciousness". The title draws a line in the sand. On one side stands the neuroscientific study of the human nervous system as it alerts and signals and responds body-wide. On the other, stands the philosophical or religious approach to human consciousness which tends to attribute something *that* uniquely influential to a specific organ or ephemeral beyond the biological realm.

When the brain becomes aware of any passing data it considers to be "survival-quality", it releases hormones and neurotransmitters that cause increased heart rate, eye dilation, trembling, goose bumps, and many other physical changes we are, and are not, conscious of. What self-awareness there is takes place in the cortex, mostly the front part over the eyes, an area that allows humans to plan ahead and cooperate in social groups. The gift of the frontal part of the human cortex is awareness of how the more primitive part of the brain is responding. That awareness allows humans to control their primitive responses for long-term benefit without sacrificing short-term safety. Don't worry, if the danger is imminently life-threatening, the cortex never hears about it;

the primitive brain systems freeze you or start you running without your even being aware of anything. The brain needs only nanoseconds to transmit a signal, such as "tyrannosaurus rex there", from the primitive limbic system to the cortex, and wait while the cortex checks past experience to make sure it is not just a cloud formation so you can go on picking bananas before it is too dark. Even so, the limbic system reacts first and leaves the thinking until later on the principal that if you stop to remember the name of something as big as a "tyrannosaurus" it is too late. Yes, emotions can get humans into trouble — from constant stress responses to a bad marriage — but survival has always been the tradeoff.

The human cortex's role in restricting the expression of emotions allows people to get along with each other, for one thing. They can then achieve long-term goals that allow them to survive. Thanks to self-awareness, individuals can choose to put limitations on their personal advantage for the protection they reap from long-term social support. Perhaps guilt is the downside of that "gift" of self-awareness. On the other hand, remorseless sociopaths often turn out to have suffered damage to the same part of the prefrontal cortex that controls emotions in favour of the future fruits of social cooperation.

We find it difficult to devise pencil-on-paper exercises for such subject matter. Appropriate emotional response and effective social interaction present moving targets that true-false and multiple choice cannot hit. This section, therefore, offers mental exercises that two people can do together. It provides scientific findings about gender differences in the human brain and it offers self-tests, one of which asks you to compare your ethics with those of business school graduates and convicted felons.

Possible Pairs

DIRECTIONS

Make seven pairs out of these 14 different items. Use each picture once and don't leave out any pictures. Pair them so that all seven are the best combinations, based on whatever similarities make most sense to you. There is no "correct" solution; some possibilities are given on the answer page.

For fun, try this one with a friend, and see if you both match the items in the same way. Score two points for each pair of yours that matches your friend's answer, and zero points for each pair that doesn't match. Twelve to 14 points: like minds. Eight to 10 points: keep talking. Zero to 6 points: different planets.

Didjaknow... EXPRESSING EMOTION IS A UNIVERSAL COMMUNICATION

Did you know that animals and humans are alike in the way they express some emotions? Dogs, apes and humans all show anger and aggression in the same way: the exact same muscles move and the face looks the same in its major features. You will certainly understand if a dog makes an angry face at you, and a dog will know if you make an angry face at him. This universal display and interpretation of anger is a physical form of communication that has evolved, yet still exists between species because it is important for survival.

Answer on page 112

HINT: *Go with your first impressions. Then turn the page upside down and pair them again.*

People-Power

DIRECTIONS

Your memory perks up when emotions are involved because the brain, which is designed to keep you alive, is equipped with sensors alert for incoming data that relate to food, sex and danger. That is one reason people are usually more interested in other people than mere facts about things. Equally important, if a new piece of data relates somehow to something already known, it is easier to remember.

On the opposite page there are two groups of statements, one of which is upside down. (Don't look at that one yet.) Read the rightside-up list.

Now cover that page and try to answer these questions without looking.

Who wore a blue dress?

Who had a small moustache?

Who painted sunflowers?

Who tried to overcome a problem?

Who won a court judgement?

Whose husband died?

Turn the book upside-down and read the other list of sentences. Cover the page and try the same questions again. Did you get more right this time? Why?

Kerry looked good in a blue dress.

Alan had a small moustache.

Mac painted some sunflowers.

Wally devoted his life to overcoming a social injustice.

David won a crucial Supreme Court judgment.

Betty's husband died tragically.

Didjaknow... **INFANTS CAN'T HELP BEING CONTRARY**

Your infant or toddler is not being wilfully naughty when she says "No" out loud while she continues to throw toys out of the playpen. Even though baby may want to please you, cognitive brain development has not matured enough to inhibit actions that provided a reward in the past. This is why you will often see a baby making an incorrect choice or action, even when she knows and can say what the correct choice is. With time, baby will learn to inhibit impulses and unite knowledge, choices and behaviour.

Jacqueline's husband died tragically.

George won a crucial Supreme Court judgment.

Martin devoted his life to overcoming a social injustice.

Vincent painted some sunflowers.

Adolf had a small moustache.

Monica looked good in a blue dress.

Reading Faces

The ability to perceive the emotions signalled by facial expressions is a social necessity. The ability to read negative expressions (anger or disgust) begins to deteriorate in the later stages of dementia.

Of these four sets of eyes, only one is a smile of sincere, spontaneous joy. Of the others, one belongs with a neutral expression, one with condescension and one with anger. Which is which?

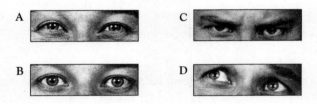

On the opposite page the full faces are revealed down the right-hand side of the page. Only one configuration of the muscles creates the *Duchenne smile* (a smile of sincere, spontaneous joy). The difference is in the use of the orbicularis oculi muscle around the eye (see illustration at right), which is the only reliable indicator of sincere joy. Do the smiling mouths on the faces down the right-hand side of the opposite page change the way you perceive the true emotion expressed?

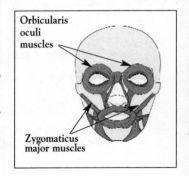

Orbicularis oculi muscles

Zygomaticus major muscles

Duchenne
smiling face

Angry face

Neutral face

Condescending face

You can make yourself feel happier by smiling — as long as you make the right *kind* of smile! Also, you can tell a sincere smile from a false smile — and, in some cases, tell an honest person from a liar — by paying attention to the muscle around the eye.

Significant Other Differences

ANATOMICAL DIFFERENCES

The human brain is composed of three major components: grey matter, where computation takes place, consists of nerve cells, dendrites, and axons; white matter, called myelin, that acts like insulation for the "wires" that grey matter uses to communicate from one region to another; and cerebrospinal fluid. While females have a smaller cranium than males (1200cc versus 1400cc), they have the same amount of grey matter as men. As cranial volume increases, men show a proportionate increase in grey and white matter, but women show a disproportionate increase: 50% of a male brain is grey matter, but 55% of the female brain will be grey matter. Why? Because woman's smaller cranium adapts by packing more neurons into it and, because there is less space, less white matter is needed to protect the "wires" since the neurons have a shorter distance to travel.

DIFFERENCES IN RESPONSE TIME

It is common knowledge that men tend to be physically bigger than women, but males also have the ability to execute motor commands quicker and more accurately than females. When asked to tap a finger during a battery of motor function tests, it was found that men could tap their fingers much faster than women. A light beam measured the tapping to ensure the difference had nothing to do with muscle strength. Moreover, PET scan studies show the cerebellum is more active in men and, since this is the area of the brain having to do with motor skills, it helps explain why men excel on tests involving motor function.

DIFFERENCE IN FOCUS

Male and female brains were studied by FMRI (function magnetic resonance imaging) while performing spatial and language tests. For both sexes, the imaging revealed a greater increase of activity in the left hemisphere for verbal problems, relative to greater increase in the right hemisphere for spatial tasks. Women appear to recruit both sides of the brain for both tasks, i.e., their brains literally race all over the place to recall an answer. This may be an advantage for some tasks. As verbal tests get harder, more regions need to be searched to find the answer. But using both hemispheres puts women at a disadvantage for spatial tasks. Because one part (the right hemisphere) of men's brains is specialized to perform spatial tasks, they perform better for that reason than women who lack a specialized area for spatial processing.

WOMEN REMEMBER VISUAL DETAILS BETTER

If you really want to know what the Jones's house looks like, it's best to ask a woman because recent tests show that women exhibit a greater visual memory than men. A group of men and women were asked to carefully study a picture of a roomful of furniture for one minute. They were then given a picture of an empty room and shown various pieces of furniture. Asked if various pieces of furniture had been in the room and, if so, where they had been situated, women remembered the items and where they were placed much better than men.

DIFFERENCES IN CONTROLLING EMOTIONAL IMPULSES

After the age of 40, men begin to lose that part of the brain that says, "Stop and think about the consequences!" Besides being responsible for abstraction, mental flexibility and attention, the frontal lobe also plays the role of the inhibiter. It is intimately connected to the limbic system, which is the emotional part of the brain, but the relationship between the two is reciprocal. While the emotional part of the brain may say "Let's, do it" the frontal part will respond:

"Wait! Think of the outcome!" Young men have larger frontal lobes than women, proportionate to body size, but after the age of 40, a man's frontal lobe will begin to shrink. A woman's frontal lobe, however, does not shrink with age.

BOTH MEN AND WOMEN HAVE TWO EMOTIONAL BRAINS ...

The emotional or limbic brain can be divided into two subsystems located deep within the centre of the brain: the limbic system and, below that, the "older" reptilian response system. This old  limbic system reacts to emotion through action, and because evolution does not throw anything away, this part still exists deep in the human brain. The second part of the emotional brain lies above it, in the cingulate gyrus of the cortex. The cingulate gyrus is new in evolutionary terms and evolved along with the brain's vocal and language areas. The new limbic system provides ways to modulate emotion by expressing it through language, making humans the only species on earth who can both act out and verbalize emotion.

... BUT THE "OLD" LIMBIC BRAIN IS MORE ACTIVE IN MEN

There's a big difference in the way men and women handle emotion, and this is especially true when they become angry. Read any newspaper and it becomes obvious that when it comes to acts of violence and aggression, men win hands down. The likelihood that a murder is committed by a man is 40,000:1 and this phenomenon is seen all over the world. It's not due to physical strength alone — firearms equalize this factor since it doesn't takes much strength to pull a trigger. While men may show anger in an aggressive, physical manner, women tend to be verbal. Men fight. Women talk it over.

 ### EMOTIONS ARE KEY TO SURVIVAL FOR BOTH MEN AND WOMEN

There are six emotions that can be reliably detected on the human face in every culture around the world — and detecting emotion in others is a key element in the survival game. The six emotions are anger, fear, sadness, disgust, surprise and happiness. Lower species, such as crocodiles and rats, do not smile. Therefore, happiness or a sense of humour is recognized as a fairly new emotion in the evolutionary scale. Happiness is the only positive emotion displayed on the human face; no other is seen. Because the evolutionary process has shown that it is more important for the survival of a species to show negative emotions, this will explain why humans display five negative emotions and only one positive.

WOMEN ARE QUICKER AND MORE ACCURATE AT DETECTING EMOTIONS

When a face is computer-morphed into the shape of vase, a woman can tell whether it is happy or sad in 30 milliseconds. It will take her 20 milliseconds more to decide whether the image is a face or a vase. Men, on the other hand, take longer to attach an emotion to the image. Moreover, PET scan studies have shown that women did not have to activate much of their brain to gauge the correct facial emotion. And even though a man takes longer, and activates more of his brain to identify an emotion, he is still less likely to come up with the correct answer.

FEAR IS AN EMOTION MUCH MORE EASILY DETECTED BY WOMEN

 There is a dramatic difference in the way men and women detect the facial expression of fear. And when men feel real fear, rather than posing with a fearful expression, women can detect the truly felt emotion much more easily. Men had a harder time identifying fear in other men, even when the man observed was actually feeling fear. And when a woman is the one expressing fear, the same result is even greater: men have a much harder time differentiating a woman's truly evoked fear from a posed fear.

MEN CAN TELL WHEN A WOMAN IS HAPPY MUCH MORE EASILY THAN WHEN SHE IS SAD

Emotional discrimination tests given to groups of men and women showed one striking similarity: women are more sensitive to happy and sad emotions expressed on the faces of men than of women. Men are also more sensitive to emotions expressed on a man's face. However, men find it more difficult to detect sadness on the faces of women. Although men are more likely to detect real sadness than a false expression of sadness, if you're a woman you cannot take it for granted that your man can always tell if you're sad just by looking at your face.

CITATIONS

P. 94 Gur, Ruben C. (1999). Sex Differences in Learning. From a presentation at the Learning and the Brain Conference, Boston, MA. November 7-9.

P. 98, 99 Ekman, Paul (1992). Facial expressions of emotion: new findings, new questions. Psychological Science 3/1:34-8.

P. 100-105 Gur, Rubin C.

olutions

CTION ONE: EXECUTIVE

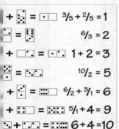

$3/5 + 2/5 = 1$

$6/3 = 2$

$1 + 2 = 3$

$10/2 = 5$

$6/2 + 3/1 = 6$

$5/1 + 4 = 9$

$6 + 4 = 10$

$6/1 + 5 = 11$

DOMI-ROWS P. 12

October and November of a year in which October first falls on a Tuesday.

S	M	T	W	T	F	S
		1			4	
		8	9		11	12
		22			25	
	28	29	30			
4					8	

FOWL PLAY P. 14

In each horizontal row, the numbers in column C equal half the difference between the

A	B	C
108	356	124
196	780	292
284	648	182

numbers in columns A and B. Thus the missing number is half of 364, or 182.

MIDDLE C'S P. 16

ASTRO-LOGICAL P. 18

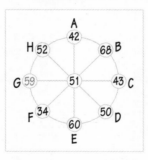

A 42
H 52
68 B
G 59
51
43 C
F 34
50 D
60
E

WHEEL OF FORTUNE P. 20

SECTION TWO: MEMORY

Theme Word:
DRAMA
1. Phyllis Diller
2. Doris Day
3. Danny DeVito
4. Robert Redford
5. Al Hirt
6. Muhammad Ali
7. Arthur Ashe
8. Dom DiMaggio Joe DiMaggio Vince DiMaggio
9. Milton Berle
10. Agatha Christie
11. Desi Arnaz

THAT'S ENTERTAINMENT P. 26

BIRTH OF A NATION P. 28

DIGIT-TALLIES P. 30

LUCKY THIRTEEN P. 32

CTION THREE: COMPUTATION

INVOICE

olley jack	£127.50
ıce	17.90
ɔotlight	24.60
	£170.00

OPS, SORRY, DICK! P. 38

WALL-TO-WALL BAGS P. 40

The entry points are 5, 7, and 8 Across, then 9 and 8 Down. The balance will come naturally.

COUNTER INTELLIGENCE P. 42

in with 5 8 Across, n 9 Down. 2 Down, first two ts could 3 or7-3; last three ld be ?-1-8 -1-6 depending on 6 Across. answer to 6 Across is 81 (any er: a too-large second digit for own, which you now know ns with 7-3). This tells you all consecutive digits are in ending order.

URATIVELY SPEAKING P. 44

Using "n" for the required number of pounds, the number of pounds times the cost per pound equals the selling price.
n oranges x 45 = 45n
20 grapefruit x 60 = 60 x 20
n + 20 mixture x 50 = 50 (n + 20)
1. 45n + 60 x 20 = 50 (n + 20)
2. 45n + 1200 = 50n + 1000
3. 200 = 5n
4. n = 40
40 pounds of oranges are needed to mix with 20 pounds of grapefruit.

NOT APPLES & ORANGES P. 46

SUMMING UP P. 48

DD-VANCE NOTICE P. 50

ADDS & EVENS P. 52

SECTION FOUR: SPATIAL

The second piece is taken directly opposite the first piece. The next piece taken is the one to the left. The next piece is opposite it; the next to the left, and so on.

A PIECE OF CAKE P. 58

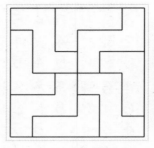

AN "L" OF A TIME P. 60

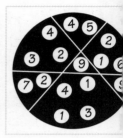

CRUNCHY CAKE P. 62

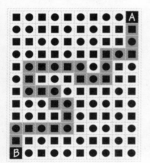

FROM A TO B P. 64

ASSYRIAN MISS-TERY P. 66

CTION FIVE: LANGUAGE

	²O	³U	⁴C	⁵H
	U	T	R	E
	T	T	E	R
	R	E	E	D
	E	R	D	S

BIZARRE ROUTE P. 72

TO	RULE	RODE	RID
LO	RILE	RIDE	BID
LA	BILE	SIDE	BIN
HA	BILL	SINE	TIN
HE	WILL	SANE	TON
BE	WELL	CANE	YON
BY	TELL	CANT	YOU

ART	ROPES	HOLE
ARE	HOPES	ROLE
IRE	HOPED	ROLL
IRK	LOPED	TOLL
INK	LOVED	TOOL
INS	LOVER	TOOK
ITS	COVER	BOOK

THOUGHTFUL BROWSING P. 74

BAH HUMBUG! P. 76

AGS	FIX		SHINE
ATS	HIT		SPINE
JTS	HOT		SPIRE
JTS	HOP		SPARE
ITS	STOP		STARE
ITS	TOO		STORE
ITH	TWO		STONE

	SAVE		
NY	SANE		CORNY
NT	LANE		CORNS
ND	LINE		CORES
OD	PINE		CORDS
OE	PILE		CARDS
OE	PILL		BARDS
NE	KILL		BIRDS

FOWL ADVICE P. 78

BESPOKE IN SPOKANE P. 80

TOTAL 340

VIOLET
VIOLE
EVIL
A VIE E
CAB I WET
BACK WHET
LACK WHITE

Colorful Conundrum Answer:

A			=	0
CAB	25		=	25
BACK	25 + 25		=	50
BLACK	25 + 10 + 25		=	60
				135

I			=	0
VIE	25		=	25
EVIL	25 + 10		=	35
VOILE	25 + 10		=	35
VIOLET	25 + 10 + 5		=	40
				135

E			=	0
WET	15		=	15
WHET	15 + 10		=	25
WHITE	15 + 10 + 5		=	30
				70

135
135
+ 70

Total 340

COLOURFUL CONUNDRUM P.82

DITCH THAT TRUCK! P. 84

N'EST-CE PAS? P. 86

A. AL GLOWS/GALLOWS
B. GRAIL MOTH/LOGARITHM
C. NEW MAID/ANIMATED
D. DEAL/LEAD
E. TRAIT/RAITT
F. AWRY/WARY
G. DUNES/NUDES
H. TIE GAL/LIGATE
I. DUAL/LAUD
J. REAL LST/STELLAR

K. SEAR TOE/ROSEATE
L. MORE VIP/IMPROVE
M. SENSITIVE/VISIT SEEN
N. TAMED ROC/MADE ROTC
O. REPUBLICAN/NEAR PUBLI
P. INDEP/PINED
Q. MED/DEM
R. CAVORTED/CARVE DOT
S. YEA/AYE

HANG IN THERE! P. 88

SECTION SIX: SOCIAL / EMOTIONAL

Left Brain Matches:
rain cloud — tornado
beach umbrella — sun
bugs — snail
top — noisy kids
igloo — house
bowler hat — beanie
crying lady — happy man

Right Brain Matches:
rain cloud — crying lady
beach umbrella — beanie
top — tornado
igloo — bowler hat
sun — happy man
bugs — noisy kids
snail — house

POSSIBLE PAIRS P. 94